Mind's Journey Through The Heart

About the Author

Nitasha Mukherji is a housewife who discovered peace and tranquility in writing. A year ago she started using this passion to write poetry and decided to present her thoughts in a way that would capture the heart of a reader. This book is a collection of 48 English and Hindi poems that would give its readers the much sought-after luxury of loosing themselves in a world that is filled with love, magic, dreams and insight.

Nitasha holds a Post Graduate Diploma in Business Management and has worked for several years before and after marriage in the field of Academics and Finance. Now she is a homemaker by choice and with a routine that is same as any mother of a 10 year old, however her eyes don't see things the way you and me do and her mind doesn't absorb experiences the way we all do. She sees beauty, miracle and magic in the rising sun, in a bird's sincere effort to make a nest, in a child's innocent smile and in an old man's wrinkled face and that's what inspires her soul to express her emotions and feelings with a new vision. Her work of art proves that we all have something special within us waiting to be explored and nurtured in our strive towards excellence and perfection in life.

Mind's Journey Through The Heart

(Poems in English and Hindi)

Nitasha Mukherji

ZB

ZORBA BOOKS

Published in India by Zorba Books, 2018

Website: www.zorbabooks.com
Email: info@zorbabooks.com

Copyright © **Nitasha Mukherji**

Print ISBN : 978-93-87456-91-4
E-Book ISBN : 978-93-87456-92-1

Zorba Books Pvt. Ltd.(opc)
Gurgaon, INDIA

Every poem that
I have written has been inspired by one or the
other person in my life
may it be family or friends or just aquintance.
They all have remarkable contribution in making
me what I am today....

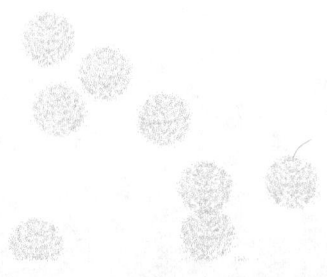

Contents

Life

When life becomes like ride on a rocking boat,
And you feel you are losing the grip on road.

The days seems like raging storm,
And nights sleep is no more a norm.

Morning sky becomes dull and dark,
Your dream's ride you're unable to park.

Golden sun keeps burning your hope,
And you seem to be pulling on an endless rope.

Dusk and dawn all covered with gloom,
Nowhere any flower seems to bloom.

All the roads start to fade and blurr,
Trust yourself and give your thoughts a stir.

Believe that you can still make a mark,
No storm can ever kill your inner spark.

Deep inside some flame is still burning,
The faith that success awaits the turning.

In the rain of light buttercups seems to bloom,
It will wash away the dark clouds of the gloom.

No more you have to run in the race,
Where you can't match the sorrow's pace.

With the light so bright at the tunnel's end,
You will find your dreams at the road's bend.

Don't feel lonely, down and lost,
'Coz he'll hold you up at any cost.

Brush the mess and plunge deep inside,
Lord is there to be your inner guide.

Distant and shallow becomes dark clouds,
When you realize you have so much to be proud.

If you keep walking and never stop,
All your failures cannot make you flop.

Its on you to always try your best,
And keep in God's hand all the rest.

You may see the whole world against you,
But the creator of it is still walking with you.

If you can hold your faith and dreams so tight,
Trust God and you will reach the destination right.

Where darkness and sorrow will have no hold,
And you will enjoy the snow even if its so cold.

Far and far will go your worry,
With fun and frolics in your life's curry.

So trust yourself and have faith inside,
And you will never lose control on your ride......

Nature's Gift

Morning sun glows in the sky,
Seeing the birds chirp and fly.

Beauty thriving in nature's lap,
With life's secret in every wrap.

Roses, lilies, daffodils and lavenders,
Bringing joy and colours to every calendar.

Watching deer galloping in rain,
All will forget their sorrows and pain.

Dazzling rainbow in the evening sky,
Almost I can see pretty fairies fly.

Stars like diamonds sparkling with the moon,
Making stream of water like dancing on a tune.

Seeing Gods peeping on us with shimmering eyes,
Who would believe in the world there are any lies.

If we nurture the beauty nature bestows,
We would see happiness and prosperity always flows.

No cries ,no struggles, no fight, no hate,
Our best guide becomes our changing fate.

With peace, calm and love everywhere,
The planet becomes a joyous sphere.

Like lightning illuminating world in the night,
Our spark of determination shines so bright.

With empathy love and stream of joy,
We play with the struggles like a toy.

Keep your passion burning so strong,
And you will never tread the way that is wrong.

Like dancing trees in harsh wind of summer,
We move ahead through struggle's hammer.

How garden blooms with flowers in spring,
Success plays on life's violin strings.

Life and death are all illusion,
Truth lies behind our all confusion.

The more we ask, the more we try,
The river of knowledge will never dry.

Till we reach and a place we find,
Where peace and truth is in every mind..

Vision

I feel your presence in the fragrance around me,
But cant reach your heart and you never see.

In flowers, mountains, rivers and sea,
I wish there were memories of you and me.

Like my heart and soul I know you in mind,
But around the world why cant I find?

The heart that I can hear beating so close,
Fades from my vision like a dream of rose.

Walking in the woods with hand in hand,
Making those castle together on sand.

Laughing on jokes that doesn't make sense,
Playing with the flowers growing around the fence.

With sparkle of dreams in dancing eyes,
We stretched our hands and touched the skies.

I feel I have lived it all in my life,
The way a gull touches water in its every dive.

The joy and bliss of it feels close enough,
Why finding it around me becomes so tough.

Like a mirage that you can see but never touch,
It runs away like a wild doe scared so much.

Seeing flashes of dream through my open eyes,
Spreading wings of imagination how high I can rise,

Near my heart and in my soul,
I could find my cherished dream and goal.

All around me the light so bright,
Burns with the passion of truth and right.

Every race and search ends here,
The flame of one ignites from where.

All I've seen and all I know,
Seems to be melting like a mountain snow.

Things I held so close and tight,
Burnt like hay in knowledge's light.

Still I feel the power burning in me,
Blooming like a petal from a cut down tree.

With every beginning and every end,
Flaws and failings are always mend.

Like sun, joy rose from fading clouds,
To cherish all the gifts as I vowed.

Like endless water in waves of sea,
And countless leaves in a growing tree.

The peace inside grows around and far,
And will never fail to heal a scar.

To My Teacher

Shading like a tree taking all the blow,
Holds through hindrances so the river can flow.

Strong like a pillar in the crashing waves,
Gives the disciple the knowledge it craves.

Showing us the path of virtuous attitude,
Kindling in our hearts the light of gratitude.

Like a sculptor carving idol from a stone,
Makes a clueless child worthy of a throne.

Will the diamond shine lying in the coal?
Lacking final guidance can we reach the goal?

When the path of success seems so bleak,
Holding our hands pushes us to peak.

Clearing all the doubts making learning fun,
Rising from horizon like a glowing sun,

Lost in the time, forgotten by the peers,
Lives in his preachings still conquering the fears.

Oh I still remember his warm and gentle face,
When I went to him like a hopeless case.

He showed me the power buried deep inside,
Patted my shoulder to express his pride.

With endless calm and patience made the path clear,
Wiping like dust all my inner fear.

Still I hold his picture deep in my heart,
Inspiring me to remember I can win if I start.

Content in the background pushed me ahead,
Like a skillful gardener nourishes roses red.

I wish I could thank him for honing my skill,
Help shaping my destiny and strengthening my will.

Mom

My dear mom what a miracle you are,
Illuminating my world like the brightest star.

Holding me up when the world pulls me down,
Absorbing all the grief without a single frown.

Love in your heart is deeper than the sea,
Helps me fight the odds to see what I can be.

Tired to the bone by end of the day,
With the last bit of strength for the kids she will pray.

Sensing my sorrow when what the world sees is smile,
Shielding my heart from the forces guile.

Hold me in your arms and make all worries fly,
Like a mass of water in a desert dry.

Greatest of my blessings and most cherished prize.
Your love will never end even if the sea dries.

Gardener's Seed

Oh my little tiny seed,
How I thought you were a bead.

Kept in a treasure box for so long,
Sang for you my hearty song.

Kept under pillow in my lovely bed,
Thought you will bloom into roses red.

Held you away from nature's treasure,
Surprised when it failed to give me pleasure.

Like moons and stars won't rise in the day,
Flame can't illuminate like sun's rays.

Tied in shackles of fear and gloom,
Hidden potential will never bloom.

Throwing it down in the lap of earth,
Challenged the seed to show its worth.

Now you are lost in mud, rain and sun,
Wasn't lying under the pillow so much more fun.

Lost your size, shape and colour,
But living through all this needs valour.

What you were and what you are,
Now I can see where you reached so far.

Breaking the shell came leaves so small,
Will you ever become a tree so tall?

With nature testing its strength and will,
How can it keep growing still?

Filled with leaves, flowers and seeds,
Providing for master's children's needs.

Never looks back what it was one day,
Will end giving others it'll always pray.

Seeing you grow with pride no fear,
How I could keep you locked my dear.

Holding with fear of losing what is,
How can you ever become like this.

Pretty like a bride with delicate flowers,
How your branches dance in morning showers.

Cherished by the world is no surprise,
Watching you thrive is my biggest prize.

Love

Love is that spark you can never conceal,
Bruised or battered souls it will heal.

Deep like the ocean and high like the sky,
Free like a bird souring so high.

Fluttering like wings of hope and joy,
Indifferent from world's treacherous ploy.

Cuddling a baby to giggle and play,
It can evoke God in an idol made of clay.

All feelings making us rise or fall,
Love is always in the base of all.

Love for jewel or love for toy,
The only thing we ever crave is joy.

Lost in the jumble of wants and need,
Monster of darkness and evil will feed.

Spreading the smoke and covering the glow,
Why do we have to let the monster grow.

Shaking off the weight of what we need,
Lets brush away the hatred and greed.

Glowing like a rising sun love will spread,
Holding all together with its delicate thread.

How much evil buries it deep and down,
Love will always wear the victory's crown.

Veiled like a treasure box inside the sea,
Waiting to sprout in hearts of you and me.

Worship of Gods and Angel's pride,
Through the perilous path it will always guide.

Racing like the fire in a forest of vice,
Healing the hearts and breaking the ice.

Smiling through the buzzing of bees on the charming
flower,
And spilling through the dance of peacock in the
summer shower.

Love will spread the peace and joy in the hearts of all,
Holding good with tender hands in people big or small.

Moon In The Sky

My dear round glowing moon,
How you become big so soon.

Rising in the sky of midnight blue,
Like a silver ball of sparkling glue.

Waves in sea rises high to touch,
The glory of pretty moon is so much.

Primerose, water lilly blooming in the night,
Watches Angels dancing in dreamy moonlight.

Spreading its light like flowing white silk,
On the smiling fairies with dresses white as milk.

Peeping from the window guarding me in sleep,
Caring like a mother in it's heart deep.

Shining in your glowing light weeping cherry,
As if God has come down on a ferry.

Making dripping dew drops look like diamond tears.
Melting like snow in sun vanishes my fears.

Sailing in the sky like a ship made of pearl,
If its not fixed I am sure it would swirl.

Struggling through the passing clouds inspiring love
and dreams,
Growing like a blooming rose always it seems.

Do the angels play with it thinking its a ball?
Can I keep it in my closet down if it falls?

I can see it smiling like a crescent jewel of gold,
Laughing at the thought that people call it old.

Glittering over the howling wolf makes a perfect snap,
Holding every writer's breath like a dove's flap.

Dreams

Dreams sweet dreams stay in my heart,
Carrying precious gems in a golden cart.

Reflecting a happy or sad mental state,
Like a tangy sauce leaving colour on a plate.

Sneaking in our sleep in darkness of night,
Bringing in its fold memories or insight.

From children's fairytale to Santa Claus's sleigh.
Miracles in dream are like a child's play.

Reliving in dreams feelings of the past,
Moments of life's journey that could not last.

Can you tell us why a baby smiles in dream?
Is it the mother cuddling or yummy ice cream?

Dreams keeps us going in times hard and rough,
Giving inspiration not to quit and be tough.

Dreams to climb the mountains, dreams to touch the sky,
Dreams can shake our doubts ushering us to try.

Dancing like a fairy in thoughts of a lover,
Twinkling in our eyes as elucidation we discover.

Traveling the world sitting on its golden wings,
Playing confounding music in our heart's string.

Holding them with hands and keeping them so close,
Keep fighting all the odds and vanquishing all foes.

Work towards the dreams n follow your inner voice,
Guidance it will give when we fail to make a choice.

Silence

In depth of the sea and heart of the earth,
During ineffable times we feel its worth.

With slightest of smiles and gloss in the eyes,
Does holding the silence always means lies?

Like a king's crown and warrior's sword,
Silence is more precious than incoherent words.

In deepest of sorrows and highest of pleasure,
It manifests best what we can not measure.

When shattered by your own deeply trusted sources,
Silence can only defeat those forces.

For the thirst that never seem to quench in life,
Can the words ever fathom the strive?

In a quiet sleep and feelings so deep,
Lost in our thoughts we can sense it creep.

When we need words assuring and warm,
Silence can be killing precipitating inner storm.

Golden in fights dissolving the rage,
But if always used becomes like a cage.

Broken by the thunder or rustling of leaves,
Rising between cries when a person grieves.

Haunting like ghosts in failing communication,
Frozen on the lips expressing frustration.

Could the wars be stopped replacing it with words,
So there were no fears in clanking of the swords.

Working like lullaby in a mother's hug,
Loud like a drum in a child's silent tug.

Reading all the mysteries only through the eyes,
Words will never reveal so much to a friend wise.

Swamped by overwhelming feelings and thoughts,
Silence will unfold the answers we sought.

Time

Moving non-stop on a tick-tock clock,
You will never see it like a ship on the dock.

Keeping in its fold good and bad memories,
Sharing with all mystery of the stories.

Sometimes moving slow sometimes moving fast,
We have to use it wisely coz it will not last.

Like a chocolate in the heat, it will melt fast,
We can never change a thing from our past.

If we don't value and acknowledge its worth,
We will fail to realize what our life is worth.

Witnessing with somber eyes all our pain,
Says we could always change it to gains.

It stays our best guide if only we believe,
Do you think it makes us stressed or relieved?

Moving like a shadow it never complains,
Even if we were lazy and missed our train.

Slipping like sand from the tight fist,
Vanishing like butterfly in the morning mist.

Do we learn its worth from tales new and old,
Haven't we read kings losing all their gold.

Do the people change or its just their time,
We wonder when we see a miser spending all his dime.

Flowing with the stories of great emperor,
And glamour of princess delicate as a fur.

Struggling in the revolutions against and for,
Crying in the bloodshed and miseries of a war.

Silently it keeps burning like a flame,
Taking our losses' and failure's blame.

How we all cherish it with ice cream in mouth,
Same becomes a burden when something goes south.

Aren't we responsible to make it all count,
Can you ride the horse if you don't mount?

Changing like seasons in perspective of all,
You can call it teacher or reason for your fall.

Fraction of it gained, fraction of it lost,
No one can escape ingnorance's cost.

Whatever you think its a friend or a foe,
Boat will only move in the direction we row.

If we miss the rain needed for a crop,
We would never know the prize it holds in every drop.

If we break a diamond shining white and bright,
Giving all thats our worth, can we fix it right?

Lost in deep worry, apprehension and thoughts,
Can we fill the life's journey's blank spots?

Like the shape of cloud is never the same,
We can never fix a lost time frame.

So live in the present, stop dwelling in the past,
What you have now, forever will not last.

Destiny's power you can never defeat,
In the rainy days what's your retreat?

Who teaches an ant to make the ant hill,
Nothing can take your time unless you will.

As the wilted rose will never bloom again,
Take a step forward forgetting past pain.

Road

Spiralling zig zag like a snake moving up and down,
Carries all rich or poor in city, village or town.

Smooth as marble, rough as gravel or shiny as a
horse's mane,
As a kid how i wished I could see it under a flying
aeroplane.

Moving along a river bank kissed by the daisies,
Or flowing silver line in the field where the cattle grazes.

Stark under the moving cars making town's street,
Or broken and cragged, lost in the jungle of concrete.

Dear to a person moving with a destination in mind,
Mean and endless, harsh and long for the lost kind.

How to know if it ever matches a racer's pace,
Or pushes him to put all the efforts maintaining its grace.

Basking under blazing sun in a summer noon,
Shaded by bending trees brightened by driver's croon.

Glowing in the rays of moon shining with glow-worms,
Does it change from day to night or alters it's terms?

Turning round and round on towering mountains,
Can it ever touch the horizon in the high plains?

Living in the memories of friends on a ride,
Swaying under the moving bus like rising tide.

How we all wish we had a road till the moon,
And the same taking us to mars in the noon.

Sunshine

Falling on my window glass shining so bright,
Makes me wait to see its magic all through the night.

Bringing life and growth to my little garden,
Bearing through the fire's heat like the gold will harden.

Touching with its magic healing poor and rich,
Clearing vision of path and breaking traveller's hitch.

Adored in the moving path of a sunflower,
Like the dedicated endeavours of a lover.

Like different streams flowing merges into sea,
Sunshine brings abundant joy, hope and glee.

Sun will reach and bless us in its every ray,
And will brighten our hearts on a gloomy day.

Every single ray in the radiant sunshine,
Has the power to evoke dreams and thoughts divine.

With the morning rays sky blooms with spectacular hue,
Dispersing all the mist dissipating drops of dew.

All the evil and darkness engulfed in its power,
Like dreariness of barren land broken by a flower.

Glittering like sapphire in evening at my yard,
Spilling like rain of diamonds through the fence's guard.

Spreading charm and hope like smile of a child,
Leaping through the shadow like a jaguar wild.

Missed on the days with gloomy thundering cloud,
Does it ever favour an individual or crowd?

Basking in its charisma in chilly winter days,
Blessed be the crop so the farmer prays.

Fighting inner darkness like a sacred shrine,
Ignites spark of hope this morning sunshine.

My Daughter My Angel

My dear cute lovely little girl,
Pretty and precious like a pink pearl.

You are the diamond closest to my heart,
Are you just a child or God's greatest art?

Naughtiness and mischief twinkling in the eyes,
I hear her dreamy stories where she can touch the skies.

Laughing and giggling together on funny jokes,
Goggling at pretty dresses like couple of college folks.

Makes me live the days of fun long lost in time.
Following me with tiny steps in my every strive.

Brightening our lives with scintillating smile,
She is the perfect reason to forget our worries for a while.

My little princess apple of my eye,
Why my heart seems to sink every time you cry?

Enriching our world with joy love and pleasure,
Worth of a daughter no means can ever measure.

The day when you'll leave the nest and fly like a free bird,
We'll cherish the memories with tears of joy making
vision blurred.

Journey of Life

What one ever learns in the journey of life,
Depends on the choices in everyday's strive.

Roots of tomorrow and reflections of past,
What we make of the present, its impressions will last.

A single seed sown will give us million seeds,
What our life becomes is impression of our deeds.

Flowing like a river or stagnant like a pond,
Its only we, who with supreme power, can strengthen
our bond.

From Innocence of the childhood to wisdom of the age,
Is every act we do, a step to that stage?

See every drop of rain as your beloved's precious tear,
Gather courage and make up for every moment lost in
inactions and fear.

Today the life may seem long, full of monotony and
tedium,
But the day you realize life's purpose, you'll see it as a
lost medium.

So lets hold on to our dreams close to our heart and tight,
And always walk the path that's virtuous and right...

My Pet

Lovely, cuddly, small pup came to my home,
Not from London, nor from Italy, neither from Rome.

Love, Innocence, and mischief twinkling in tiny eyes,
Jumping like a ball of fur trying to catch the flies.

Curled on my lap in sleep deep and sound,
Tapping around the house paws tiny round.

Squirming in my arms like a cute little toy,
He is not a pet but a bundle of joy.

Waiting to play with me all day and night,
Hope to get a yummy treat in the eyes bright.

Loyal and loving, playful and kind,
A friend like a dog we can never find.

Illustrated
by Aparna

Butterfly

Far and far away from my sight,
Like a colourful flickering light.

Come to me and settle a little bit near,
Let me touch your beauty oh! my dear.

Sit on my palm and look into my eyes,
Together lets fly high in the skies.

Give me your colours and give me your wings,
So that I can dance on blooms , petals and strings.

Show me how to take the nectar from a flower,
How you protect your colours during heavy shower?

Do you play on roses and sleep on their petals?
Do you drink the nectar boiling it in tiny kettles?

I wish i could travel to your fragrant world,
And hide in pretty blossom with my wings curled.

Earth

We live and thrive on the planet and call it our earth,
It has got so much beauty but what all is it worth?

Replacing the trees and jungles with factories
puffing smoke,
Going against the nature, misfortune is what we evoke.

Misusing limited resources and disrespecting its wealth,
Aren't we jeopardizing our own children's health?

Still in our hearts deep we crave the simple pleasures,
That smiling nature spills during rare moments of leisure.

Then why in the race of building better future for all.
We end up burying real prosperity under edifice so tall.

Care for, protect the planet and try not to cross the fences,
Or face the wrath of nature and bear the consequences.

You in My Heart

Where ever I go whatever I do,
Nothing feels complete ever without you.

Surrounding my heart, near to my soul,
Distance from you nothing can ever console.

Together we shared dreams of tomorrow,
How could you leave me drowned in sorrow?

Out in the crowd my eyes only look for you,
Waiting for that moment when I can get a glimpse or two.

Breaking all barriers fighting from the world,
Feeling your love my heart seemed to swirl.

You came in my life like a God's gift,
Then what went wrong and created the rift?

The harder I tried to hold you close and near,
The more overwhelming became my fear.

Every goal we chose every path we walked,
Forgetting day and night the way we talked.

Was every word of care only an illusion,
The joy that we felt was nothing but delusion.

Did you never utter the promises I heard?
With emotions in the eyes making vision blurred.

The farther you will go, away from my sight,
The stronger love will become, glowing more bright.

Every time I believed I've healed through my tears,
Then why does it hurt seeing I don't matter to you dear.

Though every step forward took us apart,
Till the day I live you will stay in my heart.

Who Am I

My dear lord, oh! my guiding light ,
Whatever feels wrong will I ever set it right?

In quest of the peace, happiness and joy,
Why the mind keeps building ineffable ploy.

Is it war and fight or injustice all around,
Are we all divided only on the ground?

Do mind, soul and body have distinct existence?
Why the soul keeps suffering from mind's resistance?

Hearing through the ears and seeing through the eyes,
Then why the pain always in the heart arise?

With smile on our face we welcome morning ray,
But pain in the heart still seems to stay.

Can't you ever see my inner self is more,
Than impressions that external appearances pour.

Ripples of a harsh blow whether new or old,
Makes me introspect and take a step bold.

Waiting to be seen as a human with a heart,
Ready to give up what I held from the start.

Perplexed with the differences of feelings out and in,
Failing to conquer the peace even when I win.

Draining our strengths , dispersing the energies,
From lacking in body, mind and soul's synergy.

I can only pray to my soul's guiding lamp,
One day I discover what and who I am.

Hope

Burning like campfire in a beginner's heart,
In every tale of success having a vital part.

Never leave its handle even if you fail,
As you can climb the peak however you're frail.

Like fragrance of rich coffee tingling our senses,
A single ray of hope inspires to jump all fences.

See it in the eyes of an erring child,
That he will be spared with a scolding mild.

Twinkling in farmer's eyes for the sprouting seeds,
Flashing in the racer's grip at a high speed.

Jingling like bells in worship of a saint,
Telling different stories through artist's paint.

Budding like new petals after the fall,
We should keep moving even if we crawl.

In growing of a life inside a mother,
Safe and curled inside smiling with no bother.

Hope of morning sun in winter night's sleet.
Avalanche will stop and storm will retreat.

If you lose once everything you hold,
Can you not go on a voyage to find gold.

What makes us to get a peaceful night's sleep,
Belief to see the morning sun in our hearts deep.

Sinking in the swamp, tangled in a rope,
What will life become just without the hope.

It gave me the courage to walk the darkest road,
Pushing through the hurdles till prize of victory glowed.

Arising in our hearts as dreams for tomorrow,
That we will spread the joy fighting all the sorrow.

Illustrated
figure

Cottage On a Hill

Clouds are rising up high on the hill,
Sheathing with its arms cottage standing still.

Surrounded by the woods, rocks and flowing stream,
Like a picture perfect from an artist's dream.

Leaves like emeralds on trees all around,
See the nature smiling in sky or on ground.

Smoke from the chimney mingling with the fog.
Breaking of the silence by croaking of a frog.

Dripping like crystal mist from the roof,
Quivering of the earth under horse's hoof.

The big yellow dog greeting morning sun,
Guarding old grandmother baking hot bun.

Away from the noises and crowd of the town,
Tucked in nature's lap shining like a crown.

In music of the wild and the night's chill,
Cryptic like a magic standing strong and still.

Drowned deep in peace, calm and solitude.
Shelter earning lost traveler's gratitude.

Through the journey's obscure and adventurous thrill,
Discover the mystery of the cottage on a hill.

Tears

Shed by the poor ,shed by the rich,
Incredible like spell cast by a witch.

Worth of a diamond in eyes of queen in a castle,
If shed by a pauper its seen like a hassle.

Carrying in every drop the weight of joy or sorrow,
Can it also fall in emotions we borrow.

Comes from the heart when hit by a hammer,
Lost in the crowd of success and glamour.

Holding it inside the heart turns it to fire,
Giving us the strength to achieve what we desire.

Reflecting innocence in eyes of a child,
Rebellious in miseries like a river wild.

Bursting like firework in the night sky,
Melting hearts of stone through a lovers' cry.

Falling on the ground flowers can it bloom,
Like flowing damn of tears washes away the gloom.

Expressing child's pain in a meagre fall,
Works as retreat in tragedies all.

Illustrated
by Aparna

Seeing goodness suffer do the angels cry.
Or can't find the tears even if they try.

Does it make us strong or silly and weak?
Or it clears our vision in a mission bleak?

Is it fairies crying in the form of rain,
As we shed tears expressing our pain.

With tenderness in heart , empathy in soul,
From weakness to strength can't we change its role?

Discover the Magic

When dawn and dusk, day and night,
Fate and luck don't work so right.

When we need sun comes the rain,
When we need joy comes the pain.

Grass in the wet rain catches fire,
Like a truthful speaker becomes a liar.

Sugar and honey don't sweeten the tea,
Troubles seem chasing even if you flee.

Petty hindrances you're unable to tackle,
Then what you need is a simple miracle,

In the twinkling star and shimmering moon,
Every new day is nothing but a boon.

You should see the miracle in newborn's cry.
From tiny curled fingers to twinkling naughty eye.

How we all believed our grandma's story,
Elves making colours from blooming morning glory.

Can't we see the blessing in every dew drop,
Feeling gratitude in every growing crop.

Isn't there a magic in every life born,
In the climbing sweet pea and cover of a corn.

Magic in the rising clouds born from the sea,
What becomes the luscious fruit on a tall tree.

Keep your heart open and the mystery will unfold,
Hidden in a wooden box treasure of gold.

Like the bold joyous playing of a child,
Soaring courage in the heart like an eagle wild.

Like feeble stream changes stride facing a giant rock.
Trivial becomes the impediments that once
seemed to mock.

Shining like a morning star emerging against the norm,
Standing strong like a mountain facing the storm.

Fairy

I have a big and tall tree,
which has jewels hanging for free.

I have hair I dont worry about tying,
when i ride my white horse flying.

I wish I had a water stream,
which had a flowing icecream.

A pretty house like drawing on a slate,
but truly its made of chocolate.

Where I could have my popcorn,
while sitting on a Unicorn.

I dont have to drink milk from dairy,
because I am a beautiful real fairy.

I have a dress and hat of gold,
which never becomes small or old.

I can make amazing magic,
which can fix any story tragic.

My Golden Hawk

Day and night you follow me like my shadow and a star,
Let me touch your golden wings,
and feel the magic across and far.

All the journeys and paths I walk,
You are my company my Golden hawk.

I sense you watching over me in the light
of midnight moon,
Shining regal God of gold in rising sun like a boon.

You see the storms swirling and rising in my heart, when
we both look at each other's eye,
In your silent look I see those answers hidden, with all
the world's diamonds none can ever buy.

Riding my white horse I went,
bolting through the spearing trees,
Thats when I felt you looking at me,
and the recognition made the moment freeze.

What holds us together is not a cage,
neither shackles nor a chain,
The bond is eternal deep and strong,
with one heart crying in other's pain.

Illustrated by
Aparna

From the day you set your eyes on me
as my saviour and my guide,
Every day you fill my life with inexplicable
pleasure and pride.

Pain

Its not the needle, not the prick,
not the fortune's gone bad trick,
What it is ? It's just the pain, dwelling in it,
what will you gain?

Slithering like a snake, inside the heart ,
Can it delude our minds? Is it so smart?

Feeding and growing on our complex emotions,
Creates confusing and troubling notions.

In rising fog of pain , our insight goes blind,
What does the heart feel and what reasoning can find?

Is it the beginning, halt or an end?
All that seems broken, will it ever be mend?

In this raging war inside heart and mind,
Where do we find the answer, in whom do we confide?

The spirit that fought all odds with sparkling zeal
and fervour,
Drowned in this incessant pain, have I lost it forever?

But no! I'll not believe, let the whole universe say,
Like sun fighting dark gloomy clouds,
one day I'll find the way.

This upheaval today ruling my life, smothering
my joyous spirit and soul,
One day will become a bleak memory and only in
strengthening me will have its role.

Learned Failures

What is this world? It's a war of pride,
Expects you to bend as a newly wed bride.

Learned and honoured, are these kinds,
How one ever comprehend
what's going on in their minds.

Pleasure for today, success for tomorrow,
Do they ever notice people dealing with sorrow?

Green and smooth like carpet of grass laid in
roads for them to walk,
But not even an open forum for underprivileged
to frankly talk.

Whole world should cry at their trivial troubles,
Insignificant are other's pain like some tiny bubbles.

Claims to have mastered the elusive art of living,
How one ever says so without a heart that's giving?

Wins through the trodden and weaker in power, except
any hearts coz that's not in list of pleasures,
Do we bow our heads and show them gratitude or are
they in reality called learned failures?

वक्त

कभी वक्त ने हराया, कभी हालात ने हराया,
करना जो न चाहा, वो हर हाल मे कराया ।।

इम्तिहान तो बहुत लिये जिन्दगानी ने,
पर हर इम्तिहान ने कुछ नया ही सिखाया ।।

मुकम्मल न हो सका प्यार का जहान,
जब भी तलाशा तुम्को पास तो दूर हि पाया ।।

कभी वक्त ने हराया, कभी हालात ने हराया,
करना जो न चाहा, वो हर हाल मे कराया ।।

Illustrated
by Aparna

तूफान-ए-इश्क

न पूछिये क्या इश्क है ये ऐ मेरे हमदम,
खिले मुस्कान लबों पे बनके, या बरसे अश्कों में बनके ग़म ।।

इश्क की ये दासतां ही है अजब हरदम,
ख्वाब भर दे आँखों में पर नींद आए कम ।।

महके सारी ये हवाएं गूंजे है सरगम,
हंसते हंसते याद उनकी करदे आँखें नम ।।

उनकी फुर्क़त से न बढ़कर है कोइ अब ग़म,
अश्कों के तूफानों में घिरके डूब जाएं हम ।।

डूबके ही पार हों दरिया में इसके हम,
कुर्बत में उनकी जिन्दगानी ये बीते चाहे दिन हो कम ।।

इस उन्स के आफताब से रौशन मेरा हर पल,
याद में उनकी शमा से जल रहें हैं हम ।।

साथ उनके उम्र भर भी लग रहा है कम,
जुस्तजू में उनकी सारे भूल जाएं ग़म ।।

सफर

वक्त मिले तो ज़रा वक्त से बातें कर लो,
ज़ुबां पे ना आए जो वो दर्दे बयां आँखों से पढ़ लो ।।

रखा महफूज़ गर तुमको खुदा कि रहमतों ने,
बन माझी सफर में किसी कि नांव किनारे कर दो ।।

मंज़िल

आगाज़ है या है कोई अन्जाम हमको ये बता दो,
ज़िन्दगी की राह पे मंज़िल का कोई तो पता दो ।।

चल रहे हैं , बढ़ रहे हैं , रोज़ खुद से लड़ रहे हैं,
जीत कर भी क्या मिलेगा कोई इतना तो बता दो ।।

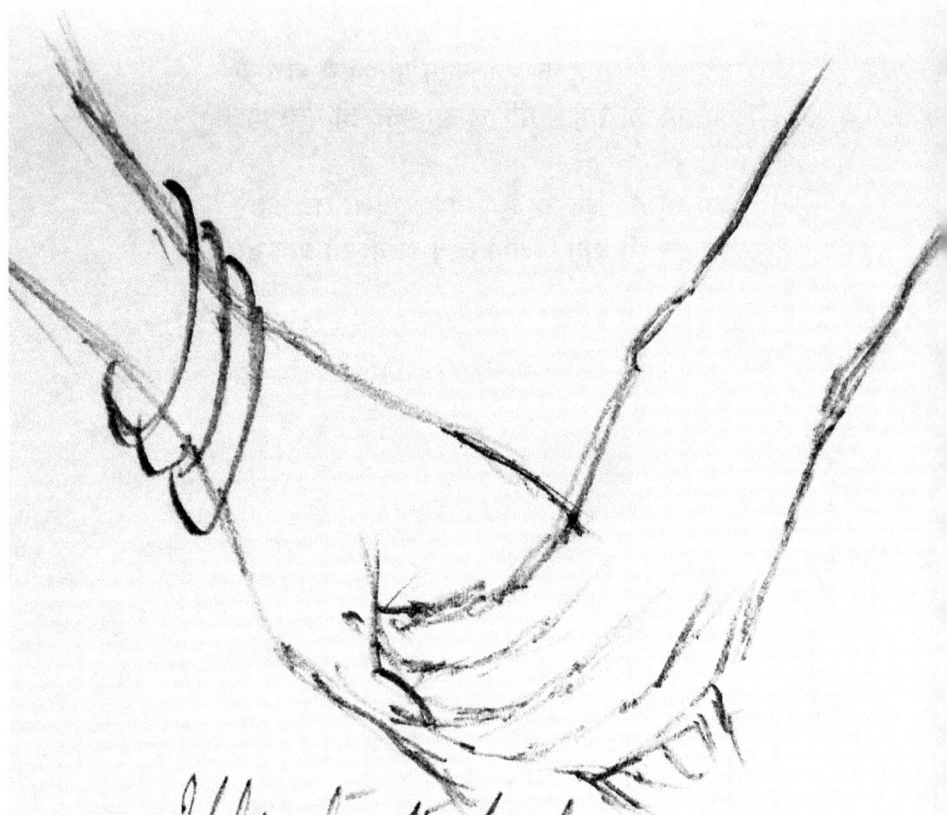

Illustrated by
Aparna

हमसफर

ख़ामोशियों में गुम हो क्यों ऐ हमसफर कुछ तो कहो,
दो हाथ मेरे हाथ में ना ग़म ये तुम तनहा सहो ।।

क्या रंज जो चलते हुये सब बुझ रहे हैं ये दिये,
प्यार से रौशन जहाँ जो साथ मेरे तुम रहो ।।

वजह

जो ये दर्द ना होता तो फिर दवा हि ना बनती,
तोड़े जो जुल्म कि ज़न्ज़ीर को वो सज़ा ही ना बनती ।।

कर दे जो बयां इश्क में रहमत–ए–यार की,
वो गीत ना बनता और वो जुबां ही ना बनती ।।

ग़र होती ना मुस्तकबिल में तेरे आने कि उम्मीद,
तो होती न शब–ए–इन्तज़ार और शाम–ए–वस्ल ही ना बनती ।।

मुमकिन

चाहे ये दिल तुझे चाहना,
मजबूर यूं के मुमकिन नहीं ।।

वाकिफ़ हैं तेरे जज़्बात से,
पर मंज़ूर-ए-दिल मुमकिन नहीं ।।

ज़र्रा जो तेरे उन्स का भी, हो मुझे हासिल कभी,
नायाब वो अहसास पर पाना उसे मुमकिन नहीं ।।

तेरी इक तबस्सुम के लिये, मुन्तज़िर थे हम कब से यहां,
पर रफ़ाक़त भी तेरा हमको अब मयस्सर हो ये मुमकिन नहीं ।।

फ़ुर्क़त

रूठ कर जो चल दिये तो जाइयेगा अब कहां,
ढूंढकर तो देखिये क्या ये फ़लक और ये जहां ।।

दिल कहीं हम सा कोई मिल जाए ग़र तो बोलिये,
राज़े है क्या ये बेरुख़ी, हमसे कभी तो खोलिये ।।

जाना हि हमसे दूर था तो पास फिर आए थे क्यों ?
दिल के आइने में अक्स ख्वाबों के दिखाए ही थे क्यों ?

फिर्दौस-ए-तख़य्युल में ख़ुदा से सज रहे थे वो कभी,
वीरान है वो आज जो अहसास रौशन थे सभी ।।

मेरे दिल-ए-बरबाद की जाती तो होगी कुछ सदा,
या राह उनके और मेरे हो गये हैं सब जुदा ?

शिद्दत

मेरी हर गुज़ारिश में तेरा ही ज़िक्र है शामिल सदा,
छूं कर तेरे तसव्वुर को होते दिन मेरे पाकीज़ा से हैं ।।

सजदे करूं हर रोज़ कि आए कभी इस राह तू,
होश में रहने न दे पोशीदा तेरे जो ये जज़्बात हैं ।।

आफरीन ये नूर तेरे चहरे पे कोई मोजिज़ा लगे,
क्या ये हवा क्या ये फिज़ा छूने को तुझे बेकरार है ।।

शाम से ही भड़क रही है दिल में चिंगारी कोई,
जलते रहना यूं तेरी याद में क्या हरपल मेरा अन्जाम है?

तेरे खुमार में खो कर हो जाएंगे यूं इक दिन फ़ना,
जन्नत भी ना मंज़ूर तेरे बिन हर खुशी नाग़वार है ।।

Illustrated by
Aparna

तेरे बिन

तुझको खो कर खो दिया है हमने खुद को भी यहां,
तेरे वजूद से ही तो ज़िन्दा मेरा अपना वजूद था ।।

थाम लेता हाथ तेरा, होने ना देता यूं जुदा,
ग़र होता इल्म वो तेरा मेरा लम्हा आखिरी साथ था ।।

तेरे बिन हर एक पल सदियों सा क्यों लगता मुझे,
बर्बादियों के आतिशों ने फूंका जो जहां आबाद था ।।

ख्वाबों का बिखरा ये महल बस है मेरा अब आशियां,
अनजां लगे हर शख़्स वो जो कल मेरा हमराज़ था ।।

मुख़्तलिफ़ बातों में ढूंढे तेरी ही परछाइयां,
क्यूं एक ही लम्हें में छूटा उम्र भर का जो साथ था ।।

हूं मुन्तज़िर कब ख़त्म हो सांसों का ये सिलसिला मेरा,
कर आज़ाद हर उस क़ैद से जो लगता मेरा अन्जाम था ।।

इबादत

ऐ ख़ुदा सुन ले ज़रा दिल से जो निकली आह है,
हम पर तू कर रहमत दिखा दे कौनसी वो राह है ।।

लड़ते लड़ते ग़म के तूफ़ानों में डूब न जाएं हम,
मिल जाए जो मंजिल-ए-बसीरत दिल में बस ये चाह है ।।

घिरती हुई क्यों ये ख़िज़ा जाती हुई सी बहार है,
लग रहा है आज कम क्यों रौशन-ए-माहताब है ।।

हाथ मेरा जो थामने भी आए तू ये लाज़मी नहीं,
ग़र्दिश में डूबते हौसले पर कब तक मेरा इख़्तियार है ?

दे जुनून कि जीत जायें हार के हसरत सभी,
या भुला दे हर इल्तज़ा को मेरी, क्या इतना तू नाराज़ है?

तेरी इबादत में है झुकते सिर सभी मौला मेरे,
फिर बंदगी पे उसकी मेरे लगता क्यों इल्ज़ाम है ?

गुफ़्तगू जो तुझसे हो तो फरियाद ये कर जाऊं मैं,
मौजूद है जब रूह में क्यों फासले दरमियान है ।।

ये दूरियां

ज़िन्दगी के इस सफर में कौन अपना मीत है,
दिल में जो तस्कीन भर दे कौनसा वो गीत है ।।

हार कर जो तेरे क़दमों में हैं बैठे दिल सनम,
सौगात हासिल यार की हो रहमतें तो जीत है ।।

अफ्सून तेरी हर अदा, अफ्सून है ये नज़र तेरी,
हैरां ही क्या जो ये हवा छूंके तुझे मदहोश है ।।

रश्क उन ज़ुल्फों से जो खेलें तेरे रुख़सार से,
हमको तो फ़क़त तेरी इक झलक ता उम्र भी दुश्वार है ।।

रूबरू जो तुमसे हों वो इक हसीन सा ख्वाब है,
फुर्क़त में तेरी दिल में उठता इज्तिराब का तूफान है ।।

हसरत में तेरी जो कहें दो लफ्ज़ भी मुनासिब नहीं,
यूं रुक गए लबों पे आके इज़हार-ए-दिल के अल्फाज़ हैं ।।

कल हर जुबां पे होंगे बेरुखी के अफसाने तेरे,
दिल से तो निकली थी सदा क्यों लब तेरे ख़ामोश हैं ।।

Illustrated by
Aparna.

मेरी नन्ही परी

ऐ मेरी प्यारी सी गुड़िया, ऐ मेरी नन्ही परी,
छिप जा तू आ आंचल में मेरे, दूर क्यों जाकर खड़ी ।।

बैठी हुई है रूठकर क्यों ये बता दे अब ज़रा,
आ दिला दूं तुझको मैं वो चूड़ियां सुन्दर हरी ।।

बाहों में लेलूं तुझको मैं लोरी सुना के दूं सुला,
महके मेरी ये ज़िन्दगी मुस्कान से तेरी खरी ।।

तेरी मुसलसल बातों से गूंजा करे है घर मेरा,
देखूं तो कितनी है शरारत आंखों में तेरी भरी ।।

रोक लूं इस वक्त को बढ़ने ना दूं लम्हे ये पल,
कल ही तो थी नन्हीं सी तू, क्यों हो चली अब तू बढ़ी ।।

महफूज़ कर तुझको मैं दुनिया के रखूं हर दर्द से,
महका करे मुस्कान तेरी बनके फूलों की झड़ी ।।

लाज़मी है कि उड़ इस आसमां में बना अलग इक आशियां,
पर दिल कहे तू छोड़कर ना जा मुझे नन्ही परी ।।

आख़री लम्हां

ठहर जा ऐ वक्त या रोक ले तू ये लम्हों का सफर,
बना ले यादों का आशियां धुंधलाते ख्वाबों के अक्स पर ।।

बंदगी में तेरी बीते हर पल मेरी इस रात का,
क्या है खबर कल सहर तक चल देंगे हम किस राह पर ।।

चाहा तो था कि साथ देंगे तेरा हम यूं उम्र भर,
नहीं इल्म था बेवफा सी होंगी सांसे ही मेरी इस मुकाम पर ।।

सोचा न था साहिल पे जाकर डूब जाएगी कश्ती यूं,
इकरार जब हंस कर किया था तेरी हर इक चाह पर ।।

पाओगे अपने क़रीब ही ढूंढोगे जब अहसास में,
पर मुमकिन नही अब साथ अपना ज़िन्दगी की राह पर ।।

कायनात की आगोश में कर दे तू अब रुखसत हमें,
आएंगे ना फिर लौट कर कोई भी हो ये चाह पर ।।

उलफत

तेरे तसव्वुर से है महकी ये मेरी तन्हाईयां,
साथ मेरा भी ना दे जब ख़ुद मेरी परछाईयां ।।

तेरी चाहत से ना बढ़कर है कोई दौलत मेरी,
हैरां क्युं तेरे नाम से फिर हो मेरी रुसवाईयां ।।

तुझसे बावस्ता वो हर अहसास दे मुसर्रत मुझे,
बयां न हो अल्फाज़ो में ये प्यार की गहराईयां ।।

तेरी आंखों की कशिश से हो गए मदहोश हम,
मुन्तज़िर है कि होगी कब हमपर तेरी ये मेहरबानियां ।।

हो भी जाएं ग़र तेरी चाहत में हम इक दिन फ़ना,
ज़िन्दा रहेंगे बनके उलफत की वो मख़फी कहानियां ।।

Illustrated
by Aparna

राह-ए-ज़िन्दगी

ऐ दिल-ए-नादां बता तू चल दिया किस राह पर है,
मन्ज़िल ये तेरी है नही उलझा ही क्यों इस चाह पर है ।।

इतनी शिद्दत से तू आगे बढ़ चला जिस राह पर है,
देख तो ऐ बेखबर जाता ये किस अंजाम पर है ।।

झांक अपनी रूह में रब का ही तो क़ासिद है तू,
महरूम इस ताकत से अपनी प्यासा खड़ा आबशार पर है ।।

मुसाफिर

हौसला न हार ऐ मेरे दोस्त, बुलंदी कि राह पे है,
डराये तुझे ग़मे तूफान , य़ा मंजिले अंजान पे है ।।

ज़रा देख तो सफ़र में कहां तक आगे बढ़ चला तू,
फिर आज यहां खोया मुसाफिर सा खड़ा क्युं ।।

क्या सूरज उगना छोड़ दे, जो आगे ना बढ़ेगा तू,
किस कशमकश में खो रहा सांसो का ये धन तू ।।

खड़ा हिमालय सीना ताने, देख बवन्डर और तूफान के आगे,
उसका ही तू आंश है प्यारे, फिर क्यों देख मुश्किलों को भागे ।।

दे हाथ तू मेरे हाथ में, उड़ चल कहीं दूर परिन्दे सा,
बसायें मिलकर फिर कहीं जहाँ शांति और अमन का ।।

महफिल

शायरों कि महफिल मे खामोश दिल तनहा सा है,
हजारो की भीड़ मे न कोई लगता अपना सा है ।।

पूछिये हमसे भी ऐ साहिब हाले दिल कभी,
या रहेंगे मुखातिब बेबाक आशिको से ही सभी ।।

लाए है सम्झाने फ़लक से नूरे खुदाई हम भी,
कि क्युं चाहिये ज़िन्दगानी मे रुलाने को ग़म भी ।।

तमन्ना

हंसे जो इक बार कोई दिल से कभी,
तो क्या कीमते सौगात फिर रोना होगा?

खिले थे फूल कि तरहा जो तमन्नाओ कि महक से,
क्या हर उस रुख्सार को आखिर आंसुओ से ही भिगोना होगा?

वो बाज़ार है ये दुनिया ऐ मेरे दोस्तों ,
जहां हर एक दिले आरज़ू को बिकना होगा ।।

क्या है उस जलते चमकते दिये कि लौ का वजूद,
सुबह कि पहली किरण पे जिसे बुझना होगा ।।

रातभर लड़के हवा, तूफां और अंधेरे से,
सुबह फिर रोशनी कि आगोश में मरना होगा ।।

तमन्ना (Part 2)

पाने को तुमहें साथ पल दो पल के लिये,
क्या इस वक्त कि रफ्तार को हराना होगा?

पूछेंगे इन हवाओं से कभी पता उस महफिल का,
जिसकी आगोश में हमें तुमने भुलाया होगा ।।

भेजकर ख़त जो तेरे दर पे ज़माने गुज़रे ,
जवाब उसका भी इस राह कभी आया होगा ।।